Original title:
The Philosophy of Pancakes and Purpose

Copyright © 2025 Creative Arts Management OÜ
All rights reserved.

Author: Sophia Kingsley
ISBN HARDBACK: 978-1-80566-148-1
ISBN PAPERBACK: 978-1-80566-443-7

Flavors Beyond the Griddle

Batter swirls and dances free,
Mixing joy with zest, you see.
Chocolate chips or berries bright,
Each bite brings a sheer delight.

Whisking dreams in morning's light,
Maple rivers flowing, quite.
Should I stack them three or four?
Pancake cosmos, I explore!

Cooking Up Conundrums

What's the meaning? Flip it fast,
Round and round, I'm lost at last.
Is it breakfast, lunch, or brunch?
I'll decide while munching crunch.

Flipping cakes like life's big test,
What's the secret to the best?
Under butter, worries melt,
With each bite, new truths are felt.

Fluffy Thoughts at Dawn

Morning whispers soft and sweet,
Pancake secrets can't be beat.
Do they dream of syrup drips?
Shall I savor every lip?

Golden circles on my plate,
Fueling thoughts, it's never late.
Do they ponder what's their role?
In my heart, they fill the hole.

Syrup and Sentience

Do pancakes laugh when I devour?
Drench them in syrup; give them power!
Do they frown when I just bite?
Or rejoice in fluffy delight?

Eating stacks with joy and cheer,
Flipping woes, let's persevere.
In the breakfast realm, oh what fun!
Syrupy wisdom for everyone!

Consciousness on the Grill

In the morning sun, I flip and twirl,
Pancakes dance, they make me swirl.
Batter sizzles, bubbles pop,
Is this enlightenment or a breakfast stop?

This golden cake, a quest for mind,
Layered flavors, treasures to find.
Maple syrup, like wisdom, flows,
Each tasty bite, the brain just grows.

Beyond the Batter

Whisking thoughts in a mixing bowl,
Batter knows the secret role.
Add a pinch of laughter, a dash of fun,
Flip those dreams till the day is done.

Stack them high, a tower of joy,
Each fluffy layer, a clever ploy.
What's the meaning? Just take a bite,
Life's a feast, and it tastes just right!

Finding Balance on a Plate

A spatula's dance, a delicate waltz,
Pancakes are peace, without any faults.
Each plate holds a story, sweet or bold,
In syrupy tales, the mysteries unfold.

Should I add berries or keep it plain?
A sprinkle of joy, or a drizzle of rain?
Life's about balance, so take a slice,
Choose your toppings, make it nice!

The Essence of Morning Delights

Sunrise whispers, time to eat,
Pancakes waiting, a morning treat.
Fluffy clouds on my breakfast plate,
Warning: this joy cannot wait!

From flour dreams to syrup streams,
Every forkful bursts with gleams.
Finding purpose in every chew,
These morning delights are made for you!

Layers of Existence

In the morning light they rise,
Soft and round, the breakfast prize.
Flip them high, let laughter soar,
With syrup dreams, we all want more.

Each layer speaks of time and grace,
A circle filled with fluffy space.
Stack them up, let joy unfold,
In a warm embrace, the heart feels bold.

Griddle Whispers

On the griddle, stories sizzle,
Golden rounds that make us giggle.
Butter melts like sun on skin,
Every flip, a chance to grin.

Whispers of vanilla sweet,
Life's a feast with every treat.
Pour the batter, make it bright,
Morning madness, pure delight.

A Stack of Meaning

A towering feast upon the plate,
Invite your friends, it's never late.
With jam and joy, we all partake,
What is life but one sweet cake?

Each bite a riddle, a tasty quest,
In every crumb, we find a jest.
Layered thoughts so light and free,
Together we unravel glee.

Golden Circles of Reflection

In circles round, we ponder fate,
As they cool, we contemplate.
With laughter loud and syruped grace,
Every bite brings smiles we trace.

Golden rounds of joy and cheer,
Flip the script, bring friends near.
In the morning's tender light,
Life's a feast, we feel just right.

Spices of Existence

In a skillet, life gets stirred,
Add some laughter, not absurd.
Flipping joy with every turn,
Sweet success we all will learn.

Maple syrup flows so bright,
Golden dreams in morning light.
Each bite shares a tasty truth,
Taste of wisdom, smile of youth.

Warmth in Every Layer

Pancakes stack as friendships grow,
Layered hearts, we bask in glow.
Syrup drizzles, hugs to share,
In each circle, laughter's flare.

Flip the griddle, what a sight,
Pancakes flying, pure delight.
Crispy edges, soft within,
Life's a feast where we begin.

Breakfast of Enlightenment

Wake up early, smell the heat,
Fluffy wonders, oh so sweet.
Every bite brings forth a grin,
Simple joys, where we begin.

Forks and knives on sacred ground,
In this meal, great truths abound.
With each taste, our minds expand,
Life's a banquet, know your hand.

Round Tables and Reflections

Gather 'round, it's pancake time,
Flipping thoughts, we share the rhyme.
Batter dreams on griddles spread,
We'll feast well, let laughter wed.

Round the table, stories blend,
Each pancake holds a tasty trend.
With syrup laughs and buttered cheer,
In this moment, purpose clear.

Syrup-Drenched Reflections

Morning light kisses the plate,
Sticky sweetness on my fate.
Life's a batter, oh so thick,
Flip it fast or it won't stick.

Maple rivers flowing free,
Pour it on, oh woe is me!
With every mouthful, truth we find,
A pour of syrup eases the mind.

Flipping Existential Dilemmas

Tossing thoughts in a frying pan,
Is this life part of some plan?
Flip that pancake, watch it soar,
What's the meaning? Who keeps score?

Do I need butter to feel whole?
Or does my heart just need a roll?
A spatula in hand, my guide,
With each flip, I take a ride.

A Stack of Meaning

Layers piled high to the sky,
Each bite whispers, 'Oh, just try!'
Whipped cream clouds and berries bright,
Search for meaning in each bite.

Do I stack or do I spread?
Questions dance inside my head.
Oh, am I empty or just full?
Life's a recipe, let it pull.

Golden Circles of Intent

Round like life, a perfect shape,
Golden promise on my drape.
Circles of joy all crispy brown,
Each one helps erase a frown.

Flip it once, or twice, for fun,
Do they ponder, or just run?
In the end, it's love we bake,
With each bite, a choice we make.

Flour, Eggs, and Epiphanies

In the bowl, a floury swirl,
Eggs on the side, ready to twirl.
Whisking dreams with a dash of mirth,
What's life without batter and girth?

Flip it over, a golden treat,
Syrup drizzles, oh what a feat!
Every bite sparks a grand thought,
In this breakfast, wisdom is sought.

The Circle of Comfort

Round and round, the pan does spin,
Butter melting, let the fun begin!
Love in each layer, stacked high and neat,
A circle of joy that's hard to beat.

With each bite, laughter erupts,
Who knew flour could build such ups?
In this warm embrace, worries fade,
A circle of comfort, blissfully made.

Essential Ingredients for Existence

A sprinkle of salt, a dash of glee,
Mixing existence, come share with me!
Baking life's troubles into a cake,
Don't take it too seriously, for goodness' sake!

Pour the batter, let it rise,
See the wonder through sleepy eyes.
A pinch of chaos, a scoop of fun,
In the kitchen, life's battles are won.

An Omelette of Ideas

Crack an egg, it's time to create,
Whisking thoughts, oh isn't it great?
Spinach and cheese, a blend so divine,
An omelette of ideas, yours and mine.

Fold in the laughter, let flavors collide,
Every omelette tells stories inside.
Serve it up warm, let's feast on dreams,
In the banquet of life, nothing's as it seems.

A Tapestry of Taste

Flipping batter with great flair,
Maple syrup drips everywhere.
In a pan, the dreams collide,
Pancakes whisper, 'Come, take a ride!'

From chocolate chips to berries bright,
Each bite a reason, pure delight.
We stack them high, a golden throne,
In syrup rivers, we are home!

Flavors of Fulfillment

Crispy edges, soft inside,
With each forkful, joy we ride.
Banana boats on sweet waves glide,
In this breakfast, we confide.

Whisking dreams with every swirl,
A tiny pancake does a twirl.
With laughter shared, and toppings grand,
We unite with batter in hand!

Breakfast Beyond Borders

In France, they fold them, oh-so-flare,
While in Japan, they rise with care.
Each country's twist, a tasty tale,
Around the world, the flavors sail.

Pancake parties, what a scene!
Toppings stacked, a feast routine.
With each bite, our mishaps blend,
And syrup drizzles, laughter sends!

Serving Up Substance

Golden circles stacked so neat,
Life's lessons wrapped in every treat.
Flour power with a side of fun,
Batter mornings, oh we've just begun!

The griddle sizzles, the toast we cheer,
With every pinch, we conquer fear.
In syrup worlds, our souls ignite,
Serving up laughs, till the day turns night!

Butter-Paved Paths

In the morning light, they rise,
Golden circles, soft surprise.
Map the syrup, sweet delight,
Fill your heart, and taste the night.

With every flip, joy does peak,
Pancakes speak where words are weak.
Slather joy, in butter's coat,
Leave the table, let's remote.

Round and fluffy, dreams unfold,
Stories linger, tales retold.
Each bite a laugh, a soft embrace,
In the kitchen, find your place.

So take that whisk, and spin around,
In pancake lands, joy can be found.
Together we'll dance, just one more round,
On buttered paths where joy is crowned.

Exploration on the Griddle

The griddle hot, my quest begins,
Map of batter, where to spin?
Each pour a galaxy, swirl and twirl,
In this round world, flavors unfurl.

As flavors mix, my dreams take flight,
Chasing sweetness, a fluffy sight.
Diving deep into chocolate seas,
Finding treasure, oh, such ease!

The spatula's a trusty sword,
Defending dreams, our common hoard.
Each sprinkle tells a story bold,
Of breakfast feasts, both hot and cold.

Let's venture forth, pancakes unite,
On this griddle, all feels right.
With whipped cream clouds, and fruit up high,
In pancake lands, we laugh and fly.

Forking the Deep Questions

With fork in hand, I ponder life,
Is syrup a friend, or a sticky strife?
To flip or fold? The question looms,
Each pancake holds a universe of blooms.

Are they breakfast? Dessert? A treat?
In their roundness, are we discreet?
Can butter teach us of love's embrace,
In every fluffy, carb-filled space?

Deep questions rise like batter on heat,
Peanut butter or jam—sweet defeat?
Let's delve deeply into this thrill,
With each bite, explore at will.

So grab your fork, let's dig right in,
To find the answers where laughter's been.
In pancake realms, we seek and share,
In fluffy waves, life's riddle laid bare.

A Side of Soliloquy

Alone I stand, spatula tight,
In the kitchen's golden light.
"Why am I here?" I softly muse,
With batter by my side, I choose.

The pancakes whisper, warm and sweet,
"Life's a journey, come take a seat."
With syrup tides, they flow and glide,
In their embrace, stones turn to pride.

Fried thoughts rise like bubbles round,
In this breakfast verse, truths abound.
Should I add blueberries or keep it plain?
Each choice a step on life's wild train.

So I serve myself, both joy and ache,
In this soliloquy, I find my break.
In every bite, the answers play,
A flavor-splashing, bright ballet.

The Alchemy of Breakfast

In the skillet, magic brews,
Flour, eggs, and sugar fuse.
A flip, a dance, a golden spin,
Why does breakfast make me grin?

A syrup river flows so sweet,
With butter clouds beneath my feet.
Each bite a potion, a tasty tease,
This morning's charm, it aims to please.

Softness and Strength

Fluffy pillows on my plate,
Wink at me and say, "Just wait!"
With every forkful, joy ascends,
Who knew dough could be such friends?

Strength in layers, stacked so high,
Wobbling like a theme park ride.
I seek soft hugs in each warm line,
A bite of laughter mixed with shine.

Chasing Flavors of Fate

A dash of cinnamon, a sprinkle of fun,
Life's a pancake race, and I'm on the run.
With maple dreams dripping above,
Each bite whispers tales of love.

Whisking hopes in a bowl so wide,
Flavors collide like a thrilling slide.
Chasing happiness, one stack at a time,
In this syrupy rhythm, we perfectly rhyme.

Fire-kissed Reflections

On a griddle where ideas sizzle,
Each pancake flips like a giggle.
Golden edges, a charming flair,
Cooking up mischief in the air.

Reflect on mornings, cozy and bright,
With sticky fingers, we share delight.
In every bubble, a secret grin,
Fire-kissed dreams, let the fun begin!

A Recipe for Being

Mix a pinch of laughter, a dash of cheer,
Stir in some syrup, make worries disappear.
Flip thoughts like pancakes, golden and round,
Stack dreams high, let joy be found.

Add a dollop of whimsy, a sprinkle of play,
Taste the sweetness of each quirky day.
In this griddle of life, be butter, not jam,
Sizzle with purpose, go do who you am.

Pouring Truths

Pour out your secrets, let the batter flow,
Add a splash of honesty, let the truth glow.
With each swirl of flavor, let your heart sing,
Life's a breakfast feast, savor everything.

Whisk together moments, blend bold and sweet,
Ketchup on pancakes? No, that's just defeat.
Flip those doubts over, don't let them stay,
Squirt some laughter, make the mundane sway.

Spatulas and Souls

A spatula's more than a flipping tool,
It scoops up dreams, like a wise old fool.
With each scrape and turn, find your groove,
In the chaos of frying, let yourself move.

Slap that batter down, hear the sizzle speak,
Life's messy and tasty, don't be meek.
And when the smoke rises, just wave it away,
Season with humor, brighten your day.

The Art of Flipping Life

Flipping pancakes is like flipping fate,
Sometimes they stick, sometimes they great.
With a flick of the wrist, dance through the heat,
Life's a brunch party, oh what a treat!

Douse those creations with laughter and glee,
Each golden circle brings you to be.
So grab your spatula, let's take a chance,
In this buffet of living, let's all do the dance!

Confection of the Mind

In a world where syrup flows,
Thoughts rise like pancakes, who knows?
Flattened by logic, but round with flair,
Whipped cream emotions rise in the air.

Toppings like chaos, decisions run wild,
Butter of brilliance, untouched and mild.
Flip the notion, it's all in the heat,
Serve up a smile, and life is sweet.

Human Nature in Layers

Life's a stack, one layer so fine,
Topped with laughter and sometimes whine.
Flip the routine, don't stick in a rut,
Even burnt edges can taste quite the nut.

In every bite, there's joy and surprise,
Under the syrup, the truth never lies.
Some days we're fluffy, others we fall flat,
Yet here we are—imperfect and pat.

Batter and Being

Mixing it up, oh what a blend,
Batter of life, on you we depend.
Pour out the worries, let griddle sparks fly,
Eat up the moments, oh my, oh my!

Flipping our thoughts, we can't be too shy,
Dreams rise like bubbles, up to the sky.
With laughter as syrup, and friends on the side,
We gather our plates, and let joy abide.

Maple Dreams and Life Streams

In the syrupy streams where dreams take a ride,
Pancakes of passion are never denied.
Maple's sweet whispers remind us to play,
Pour out the love, let it drizzle and sway.

With a dash of the silly, a pinch of the bold,
Life's griddle sears stories that never get old.
So stack up your goals, don't let them fall flat,
With every sweet platter, let laughter be fat.

The Maple Thread of Destiny

In a skillet so warm, dreams start to rise,
Flipping circles of joy, much to our surprise.
A splash of syrup, a dollop of cream,
Life's sweetest moments, a breakfast themed dream.

Batter whispers secrets, in spatula's grip,
Each bubble bursting, a promise to flip.
Oh, fate is like syrup, slow to descend,
Yet doughy delights, on which we depend.

Blueberries scatter, like stars on a plate,
While laughter and crumbs share secrets of fate.
With a fork in my hand, I ponder and chew,
The meaning of life—and the toast, too!

So gather your friends, let's pancake our way,
Through syrupy laughter, let's savor the day.
For in each golden stack, a tale to unfold,
Of syrup and dreams, and the joy that they hold.

Fork and Knife Epiphanies

With a fork in my hand, I ponder the scheme,
Can breakfast really unravel my dream?
Each cut into fluffy, warm, golden bliss,
Reveals more than syrup, but moments to kiss.

The knife lines the edge, it's sharp and it's true,
Slicing through life's layers, a taste to pursue.
With each bite I take, insights sneak in,
Like butter that melts, letting laughter begin.

Are we mere ingredients in this wonderful pan?
Twirled into sweetness, part of the plan?
Jokes dribble down like syrup on stacks,
Epiphanies rise as we sit and relax.

So when life gets tangled, just flip it with flair,
Serve purpose with pancakes, laughter to share.
A buffet of dreams, piled high on the plate,
Fork and knife wield wisdom, let's celebrate fate.

The Quiet Art of Cooking Up Purpose

In the hum of the kitchen, pans clang and sing,
A chorus of batter, what joy will it bring?
Each whisk of the egg, a gentle embrace,
Frying up purpose, each flapjack, a trace.

A sprinkle of laughter, some warmth from the griddle,
Life's flavors blend in, as we dance and diddle.
Mapping out moments with floury hands,
Tasting the sweetness of life's little plans.

Stirring up dreams in a bowl of delight,
Pancakes like clouds rise, all fluffy and light.
A dash of absurdity, a hint of wise cheer,
In this quiet art, our intentions are clear.

So let's flip those pancakes and savor the smell,
Finding our purpose with syrup to quell.
For in each little morsel, we find our way through,
Cooking up joy, life's recipe true.

Breakfast at Dawn: Finding Clarity

At dawn's gentle whisper, the kitchen awakes,
Pans dance 'neath the sun, as breakfast partakes.
The coffee brews strong, as ideas take flight,
While pancakes emerge, fluffy pillows of light.

Each sizzle and pop brings the day's first delight,
Flipping thoughts like pancakes, oh what a sight!
The syrupy glisten, a metaphor clear,
Life drizzled with sweetness, to hold ever near.

Gather 'round the table, share stories and laughs,
In this sacred space, we unearth our paths.
For breakfast at dawn is more than it seems,
It's clarity served fresh, fulfilling our dreams.

As laughter fills plates, and forks dance about,
We discover together what life is about.
So rise with the sun, with pancakes in hand,
Finding clarity, together we stand.

The Secret Ingredient of Joy

In a pan, they swirl and spin,
A dance of batter, let the fun begin.
Flip them high, don't let them flop,
Joy's a pancake, make it pop!

Syrup rivers flow so sweet,
A drizzle here, that looks real neat.
Giggles rise with every bite,
Stacked up tall, it's pure delight!

Whisk your troubles, beat them down,
In pancake stacks, we wear the crown.
Each fluffy layer hides a chuckle,
Digging in, forget the struggle!

With fruit and cream, a topping spree,
A breakfast dream, just let it be.
Laughs are best with butter spread,
Joy's a pancake, served in bed!

Nourished by Questions

Why do pancakes make us giddy?
Will syrup dance or get all drippy?
Flip, flap, flip, they crack a smile,
Ask away, stay for a while.

Can a pancake teach life's lessons?
In every layer, are our confessions!
Stack them high with hopeful dreams,
Each bite whispers: life's not as it seems!

What's in the mix? Is it magic or skill?
A dash of laughter, a sprinkle of thrill.
Questions bubble, brown and crisp,
A plate of wisdom with every wisp!

Are they breakfast or a slice of fun?
When topped with joy, they're never done.
Gather round, let curiosity rise,
Pancakes and questions, a tasty surprise!

Culinary Contemplations

In the kitchen, thoughts can twirl,
A pancake toss, a dizzy whirl.
Flour clouds with giggling throngs,
Together we'll make the silliest songs!

Is it a cake or is it flat?
A circle of happiness, imagine that!
Butter melting, syrup run,
Culinary art? Now, that's fun!

What's the secret to this delight?
A sprinkle of laughter, morning light.
With every flip, new dreams arise,
In pancake form, life's sweet surprise!

Stack them high and take a bite,
Culinary joy feels just right.
As flavors blend, let worries cease,
In a world of pancakes, find your peace!

Pancakes of Perception

What do you see? A breakfast treat?
Or layers of thought, both fluffy and neat?
Gaze a bit closer, what do they show?
Pancakes reflect what we hardly know!

Do they symbolize our daily grind?
Or maybe laughter, perfectly designed?
Flip the pancake, change your view,
Every layer has a story to construe!

Perhaps it's simple, just joy on a plate,
Or a riddle wrapped up, isn't that great?
Dig in deep, find what you seek,
In pancakes of hope, we're never weak!

Perception's sweet, just like syrup's flow,
A mirror of life in a golden glow.
Pancakes may serve on a morning bright,
But they offer perspective, day and night!

Circular Journeys: A Culinary Quest

In the kitchen, round and bright,
Flipping dreams into the light.
Syrup rivers flowing wide,
On a plate, our hopes we hide.

Batter bubbles, laughter flows,
Chasing tales as everyone knows.
Round we go, a delicious dance,
Each flap leads to a new chance.

A spatula as our guiding star,
Guiding us to places bizarre.
From flour floors to maple skies,
Each bite holds sweet surprise.

So gather round for the quest complete,
With every layer, life's a treat.
We're all sweet, in our own way,
Let's flip the script, and seize the day.

The Heat of Ambition

On the griddle, the heat does rise,
Dreams are tested under watchful eyes.
Golden edges, crisp and fine,
Ambitions sizzle, oh how they shine!

Batter mixes with a playful cheer,
Whisking doubts and stirring fear.
In each swirl, a vision grand,
What will flip, what will stand?

With every bubble, plans may burst,
Yet sweet rewards are quenched with thirst.
To stack them high or let them flop,
It's a race that never stops.

So seize the spatula, take your fate,
Spin it wildly, don't hesitate.
For in this game of rise and fall,
The heat of ambition unites us all.

Flavors of Fate

In a world of tastes, oh what a blend,
With each pancake, new paths we send.
Chocolate chips or berries bold,
Each choice a tale waiting to be told.

Cinnamon dreams sprinkle the air,
Maple whispers, sweet and rare.
With every bite, fortunes collide,
In the dance of flavors, we take pride.

Toppings piled, a mountain high,
What's your flavor? Give it a try!
Through laughter and crumbs, we find our way,
In the kitchen, we play all day.

So gather 'round this joyful plate,
In flavors rich, we celebrate.
For every pancake spun with grace,
Holds a sprinkle of fate in our space.

Pouring Truths on a Plate

Pour it thick, pour it light,
Each drop a truth, each bite delight.
Around the table, stories flow,
With pancakes stacked, we steal the show.

A splash of chaos, a dash of cheer,
Every syrupy smile draws us near.
Life's a mix; pour with flair,
On this plate, our hearts we bare.

Underneath each fluffy dome,
Lies a tale, a sense of home.
Sharing laughter with each slice,
Who knew that pancakes could be so nice?

So take a fork and make a scene,
Pour your truths, keep it keen.
In the warmth of breakfast fate,
We find our purpose, serve it straight.

Soft and Steamy Insights

Fluffy discs of golden glee,
Twirling in syrup's sweet decree.
They ponder life with butter bright,
As I munch deep into the night.

Each bite a giggle, soft and round,
With every flip, wisdom's found.
They whisper secrets, warm and light,
In the kitchen, laughter takes flight.

A spatula's dance, a joyful tease,
Cooking chaos, the perfect breeze.
Thoughts rise up like batter stirred,
In pancake bliss, dreams are heard.

So let us savor this glorious feast,
For pancake joy can never cease.
With each bite, we both explore,
The fluffy wonders life has in store.

Transcending the Ordinary: A Culinary Metaphor

Circular wonders stacked high,
Like hopes and dreams ready to fly.
And as the syrup flows like fate,
I ponder why we all await.

Golden layers, wisdom served,
In each flipping, joy preserved.
Glimmers of laughter dance on plates,
While self-reflection patiently waits.

The pan sizzles, my thoughts align,
With every pat, a spark divine.
I muse on purpose, soft and clear,
As pancakes grace me, drawing near.

So let's flip life with spatulas bold,
Create sweet moments, let stories unfold.
In batter and dreams, together we rise,
Chasing life while the butter flies.

A Slice of the Universe

In a skillet, galaxies swirl,
Planetary pancakes begin to twirl.
With each bite, the cosmos sings,
A toast to life and all its wings.

Precise measurements, a dash of fun,
Twinkling moments, one by one.
Flattened dough as endless skies,
Yeast of wisdom, that never lies.

My breakfast plate, a world profound,
With every slice, joy is found.
From butter moons to syrup streams,
Life's a dance of fluffy dreams.

So let's flip joy like pancake stars,
Topping our lives with sweet avatars.
With giggles and syrup, may we embrace,
The deliciousness in this vast space.

Breakfast for the Soul

Morning greets with soft delight,
Pancakes gleaming in the light.
With a sprinkle of laughter, start the day,
Making grumpy clouds drift away.

On the table, treasures stack,
Batter hugs that warmly pack.
A side of fruit, a dash of fun,
Every pancake, a party begun.

Sizzling stories smoke in the air,
A sprinkle of joy, beyond compare.
Each bite a hug, a slice of cheer,
Warming hearts, drawing us near.

In golden circles, our dreams unfold,
As syrup cascades in tales retold.
Breakfast for the soul, we toast,
In pancake bliss, we're the most!

Drizzled Insights

In butter's warm embrace we find,
A sizzle here, a flip combined.
With syrup rivers flowing sweet,
We ponder life while taste buds greet.

Each layer stacked with dreams anew,
A fluffy stack, our pleasures grew.
Do toppings hold the secret key?
To unlock joy? A mystery!

Beneath the griddle's watchful eye,
We laugh and flip, not asking why.
In every bite, a lesson swirled,
Pancakes rule this messy world!

So grab your fork, let's take a stand,
With batter and joy at our command.
Philosophers of breakfast cheer,
As laughter thickens like the smear!

Breakfast as Metaphor

Each morning dawns, a golden chance,
To whisk away our wobbly dance.
With flour clouds, we start anew,
And batter bowls, where dreams ensue.

The eggs we crack, a leap of faith,
Like life's choices dressed with wraith.
Do we scramble, fold, or fry?
In pans of fate, we laugh and cry.

Maple drips like thoughts should flow,
Sticky smiles begin to grow.
Let's stack our cares, then take a bite,
For joy is found in morning light.

So toast the day with whipped-up cheer,
In breakfast rituals, friends draw near.
Metaphors in syrupy hues,
Life's sweet moments, let's not refuse!

Gastronomy of Existence

In every pancake, tales unfold,
Of syrup secrets, bright and bold.
We flip and serve, with wondrous flair,
And giggle at our culinary affair.

The spatula grins, a lively sidekick,
Together we concoct our magic trick.
With whipped cream clouds and raspberry dreams,
We savor flavors bursting at the seams.

Is life a pancake waiting to rise?
Or just a mess beneath sweet skies?
The art of breakfast, quirky and grand,
Mixed with laughter, it's simply unplanned.

So gather 'round, let's share our feast,
On laughter's plate, we'll never cease.
Existence served on a warm griddle,
In bites and giggles, we solve the riddle!

Cooking with Consciousness

In every flip, a mindful gaze,
As batter thickens, we ponder ways.
With each new recipe we chase,
We find our soul in every place.

A sprinkle here, a dash of zest,
We learn to savor, and to jest.
The kitchen buzz, a dance of fate,
In pancake philosophy, we celebrate!

Let's melt some butter, spread the cheer,
For breakfast gatherings draw us near.
Crispy edges, soft inside,
With laughter's warmth, we all abide.

So whisk your dreams, and pour them high,
With syrup wisdom, let's not be shy.
In cooking boldly, together we strive,
For consciousness thrives when flavors arrive!

Pans and Paradoxes

In a skillet, truths flip and swirl,
Batter meets batter, a doughy whirl.
Are we just breakfast or cosmic fate?
Spatulas ponder our existential state.

Syrup flows like deep thoughts in time,
Sweetness and sorrow, or pancake rhyme?
Each bite is a question, thick like a dream,
Maple syrup drips, or is that just steam?

Baking in circles, we round and round,
The answer's there, but it can't be found.
Are we breakfast beings, or crumbs in the void?
In every small bite, a mystery deployed.

So grab your forks, let's get absurd,
Chew on the universe, not just the curd.
In this kitchen of life, let laughter reign,
Pans and paradoxes, let's flip the mundane.

Sifting Through Understanding

Flour dust dances in morning light,
Each granule holds wisdom, fluffy and bright.
Sift through the chaos, let logic arise,
In every fine layer, a truth in disguise.

Eggs crack open, like ideas unplanned,
Yolks run like thoughts that slip through your hand.
Whisking up wonder, we blend and we stir,
In the pot of existence, we pause to confer.

Batters collide in hilarious ways,
A dash of confusion, a pinch of malaise.
It's not just the taste; it's the mess that we make,
Each pancake a lesson, each flip a mistake.

So let's raise our spatulas, high to the sky,
In this wacky kitchen, we laugh and we sigh.
Sifting through life's flour, we find our delight,
In fluffy creations, our purpose takes flight.

Served with a Side of Wisdom

When pancakes are served, wisdom's on the plate,
Golden and crispy, they challenge our fate.
A side of confusion, with syrup aplenty,
Life's questions smothered, sweet yet empty.

Bite into laughter, a sprinkle of fun,
Why is this pancake more than a bun?
With each soft mouthful, reflections arise,
Doughy delights wrapped in humorous lies.

Flip it again, the joke's on me,
What do pancakes know that I cannot see?
In this breakfast banquet, we search for a clue,
Are we just pancakes, or are pancakes us too?

So gather your friends for a feast of thought,
With each bite we ponder, not one should be bought.
Served with a side of wisdom, we cheer,
In flavors of laughter, our purpose is clear.

Nectar of the Ordinary

In a world of pancakes, the ordinary shines,
Drenched in syrup, our chaos aligns.
A dollop of jelly, a whirlwind of jam,
Life's sweetest nectar, who gives a damn?

Fluffy like dreams on a weekend morn,
Each bite brings laughter, from chaos we're born.
Smiles between bites, that's how we thrive,
In the nectar of mornings, we dance and we jive.

Toppings galore, a savory sight,
Let's stack our hopes and enjoy the bite.
A sprinkle of zest, a pinch of the silly,
With pancakes around, life's never too frilly.

So raise your forks high, let the fun commence,
In this breakfast adventure, we embrace the dense.
Nectar of the ordinary, so rich and profound,
In every pancake moment, joy can be found.

Mindful Morsels

Flipping dough with joy in sight,
Syrup rivers, pure delight.
Stack them high, let worries cease,
Pancakes dance, they find their peace.

Griddle hot, the batter sings,
Butter melts, oh sweetened things!
Laughter bubbles, moments warm,
Flipping life, we find the charm.

Each layer holds a secret sweet,
A breakfast blend that can't be beat.
With every bite, a giggle blooms,
Savor life, in pancake rooms.

Whisk away the troubles near,
Pour some joy, and spread good cheer.
Before you know, they disappear,
Mindful morsels, bring us here.

Folding Dreams Into Reality

Whisking wishes, heavy sighs,
In a bowl, ambition lies.
Fold it gently, hopes arise,
Like fluffy dreams in sunny skies.

Pour the batter, let it flow,
In the pan, let magic grow.
A sprinkle here, a dash of fun,
With every flip, our work is done.

Pancake stacks, a mountain high,
Topped with fruit, we reach the sky.
Each bite a hug, a warm embrace,
Find your joy in every space.

So grab a fork, don't hesitate,
Nourish dreams, unlock the gate.
With laughter sweet and syrup's kiss,
Folding dreams, you can't miss.

The Taste of Time

Mornings come with buttered light,
Pancakes round, a joyful sight.
Stack them high or spread them thin,
Each warm bite, let smiles begin.

A drizzle here, a sprinkle there,
Time tastes sweeter, without a care.
Memories stir as pancakes bake,
Nostalgia served on a warm plate.

Conversations over breakfast cheer,
With pancakes near, there's love to share.
Each forkful whispers stories told,
The taste of time, pure joy unfolds.

So savor each delicious bite,
In every flipper, find delight.
Life's a feast, let's all partake,
In laughter, love, and pancake cake.

Cooking the Canvas of Life

Life's a canvas, smeared with joy,
Pancakes painted, oh what a ploy!
With a splash of color, a touch of flair,
We mix our dreams with love and care.

Griddle hot, the art is bold,
Syrup drips like stories told.
Brush on smiles, let laughter spread,
In each round cake, our souls are fed.

Whisk away the doubts we own,
The batter stirs, our hearts have grown.
A masterpiece with every flip,
A joyful dance, a yummy trip.

So gather 'round this tasty scene,
With every slice, we chase the dream.
In the art of brunch, we unite,
Cooking life, we get it right.

Griddle Dreams and Identity

In the morning light, I flip and fry,
Tossing thoughts like batter, oh my!
Do I define my worth by the shape I make?
Round and fluffy, or flat like a lake?

Each pancake whispers, 'You're more than your stack,'
Yet syrup dreams pull me down the track.
A sprinkle of humor, a dash of delight,
Who knew breakfast could begin such a fight?

The spatula's my sword, the skillet my throne,
In this kingdom of carbs, I'm never alone.
With laughter aplenty and maple to pour,
I'll conquer the griddle, forever explore!

So I serve up my truth, with a side of jam,
Flipping my faith, hoping I'll not slam.
Embracing the chaos, I dance with my fate,
For each layer I add, makes my story great!

Sweetness in Suffering

A pancake's not whole without syrupy tears,
We laugh through the mishaps, we minimize fears.
Burnt edges and lumps don't spoil the delight,
It's the sweetness in struggle that makes it just right.

Whisking my worries, I batter my doubts,
Life's got its lumps, but that's what it's about.
Cooking up courage, I flip and I twirl,
Every failed attempt makes the next one unfurl.

So pass me the berries, the cream, and the smile,
We'll feast on our failures, it's worth every mile.
In grief and in joy, we'll pancake our way,
Finding life's sweetness in all the cliché!

With laughter as topping, we'll rise from the pan,
Each flapjack a story, each bite a new plan.
So let's drizzle with joy, and garnish with glee,
In this kitchen of chaos, we're forever set free!

Layers of Life's Batter

Life's a batter, thick and creamy,
Blend in secrets, it gets steamy.
Each layer we create tells tales of the past,
In this fluffy concoction, our memories cast.

Sifting through dreams with a pinch of salt,
The pancakes of life are never at fault.
Keep stacking them high, till they tumble down,
Each syrupy spill brings a giggly crown.

I've got the eggs, and the whisk is my friend,
By flipping these cakes, I begin to transcend.
Pouring on sauce, it's a sweet covering for,
The mess that we make, who could ask for more?

So let's bake our ambitions, and fry up some fun,
Life's griddled conundrums are never all done.
With laughter and batter, we dance through the heat,
Finding joy in the layers, life's syrupy treat!

Finding Solace in Syrup

In the chaos of mornings, there lies a sweet balm,
Golden syrup pouring, it feels like a charm.
I drench all my worries, let them soak in the heat,
In the embrace of a pancake, life's struggles retreat.

Fried to perfection, they cushion my fall,
As I wobble through life, like a pancake ball.
With laughter as syrup, we'll stick and we'll slide,
Finding joy on our plates, let's savor our ride.

A spatula's dance, a flick here and there,
Crispy around edges, soft love in the air.
So gather your friends for this breakfast game,
In the syrupy solace, we're all just the same!

Through laughter and batter, we find our sweet ground,
Embracing each moment, our hearts will rebound.
So hold up your plates, let's toast to our fate,
With pancakes and syrup, life's never too late!

Batter Up: Questions of Existence

Is the pancake round, or am I just high?
Flipping thoughts like batter, do we ever try?
Do syrup rivers run in the depths of my mind?
Or are they just sticky tales that I'm trying to find?

What's the point of a pancake, so light and so wide?
Is it more than a breakfast, or just a fun ride?
Each stack like a journey, layered and neat,
Is life just a brunch, with a side of sweet treat?

In the skillet, I ponder, while bubbles arise,
Do pancakes have wisdom, or just golden pies?
Like flipping philosophies on plates they reside,
In search of truth, I don't want to slide!

With each mouthful of joy, I question my fate,
Can batter hold secrets, or just serves to sate?
In this fluffy distraction, I find my delight,
As I chew on the meaning, what's wrong feels just right!

The Art of the Fluff

In a bowl of confusion, I mix up my dreams,
With a dash of ambition and sweet, syrupy schemes.
Do eggs hold the essence, or is it just flair?
Whisking them gently, does life seem more rare?

Bubbles in batter, like thoughts on the rise,
Each flip is a chance to uncover the prize.
Is it breakfast or brilliance that graces my plate?
In the art of the fluff, I'm never too late.

Pancakes like clouds, will they lead us astray?
Or serve up reminders of what's fun in the fray?
Flipping through moments, from dawn into noon,
Eating joy by the forkful, I dance to the tune.

Laughter is fluffy, like whipped cream on top,
As syrup cascades, I just can't seem to stop.
In this simple delight, I find wisdom untold,
With each bite of the fluff, life's laughter unfolds!

Whisked Away Thoughts

With a whisk and a grin, I stir up my fate,
Do my thoughts float away, like pancakes on plate?
A swirl of color, a splash of delight,
In the kitchen of dreams, it feels oh so right.

I sprinkle in worries, watch them dissolve,
In the heat of the skillet, my queries evolve.
Are these fluffy wonders the answers I seek?
Or just morning musings, both silly and weak?

Fried on the griddle, are dreams meant to stick?
Or do they slide off, like a pancake gone quick?
Each flip brings a giggle, a chuckle of cheer,
As I ponder existence with each happy tear.

In syrup-soaked moments, my heart feels so light,
With giggles and butter, the world seems just right.
As I savor each bite, life's purpose in sight,
In whisked away thoughts, everything shines bright!

Nourishment in Every Bite

Every forkful is joy, with laughter entwined,
Are pancakes our soulmates, or just food, well-defined?
In sweetness we gather, with stories to share,
Each bite is a giggle, a delicious affair.

Do pancakes have meaning, or just fill the void?
In breakfast debates, are we blissfully buoyed?
With butter like dreams, melting time into fun,
Life is just fluff, until breakfast is done.

Stuck in a batter, we rise and we fall,
In syrupy tangents, we question it all.
Is the best part the flavor or laughter we find?
In the art of good eats, true purpose entwined.

So when life gets heavy, let laughter ignite,
With pancakes around, everything feels right.
In nourishment deep, there's a banquet of glee,
Each bite tells a story; we're hungry and free!

Browning with Intention

In the skillet, dreams unfold,
Flipping high, brave and bold.
Golden circles dance with glee,
Toasting breakfast joyfully.

Syrup rivers flow like fate,
Sticky paths that celebrate.
Each bite a quest for the divine,
Map of flavors, sweet design.

The butter melts, a silent cheer,
Whispering secrets, oh so clear.
Pancake wisdom in a stack,
Life's simple pleasures, no turn back.

So raise your spatula, give a wink,
Life's a batter, don't you think?
Flip your worries, let them whirl,
In a pancake world, watch them twirl.

A Sip of Whipped Reflection

Whipped cream clouds on coffee's dawn,
Sip and smile, let troubles be gone.
In fluffy folds, there lies a truth,
Grinning forks of innocent youth.

A sprinkle of laughter, a dash of zest,
Finding joy in a fluffy quest.
This breakfast feast has a twist,
Each bite a giggle, a shared bliss.

Current worries, a distant sigh,
As syrup cascades, we're flying high.
Mornings wrapped in sweetness rhyme,
In pancake dreams, we waste no time.

So gather friends, let's share the plate,
With every flip, we celebrate!
In life's great recipe, join the fun,
Pour your hearts out till the day is done.

Taste and Introspection

In the kitchen I ponder, flour in the air,
Eggs and milk in a bowl, life's woes I can share.
Batter thick like my thoughts, whisking it right,
Flip it over with laughter, what a delight!

Golden brown dreams, stacked high on a plate,
I take my first bite, fate's on the slate.
Do these sweet circles hold answers I seek?
Or just sugary nonsense and syrup so thick?

Savoring the Present

A fork in my hand, adventures on a griddle,
Sizzle of joy, life's comic riddle.
Each bite a giggle, syrup flows like prose,
Chewing on moments that nobody knows.

Breakfast is here, let's make it a feast,
Skipping the worries, let laughter increase.
With whipped cream clouds, it's all pure delight,
Pancake philosophy shines so very bright!

The Weight of the Syrup

Pour it thick, don't hold back, let it drizzle and flow,
Its weight on my stack makes my worries less grow.
Sticky decisions, but oh, how they stick,
Halfway through breakfast, I'm getting the kick!

Maple dreams dancing on my golden cake,
Each sweet encapsulation, a choice I can make.
While pondering life, the syrup does drip,
I laugh at the chaos, take another big trip.

Pancakes in the Morning of Life

Morning unfolds, with syrup 'neath sun,
A plate full of joy, let the feast have begun.
With laughter and butter, we dance at the table,
Life flips like a pancake, if we're willing and able.

Golden circles greet me, in tender embrace,
Drowned in sweet nectar, I find my own space.
Questions are plenty, yet I'm feeling quite free,
The morning's a mess, but it's just meant to be!

Sweetness Beneath the Surface

Flapjacks piled up high, oh what a sight,
Golden edges gleam in the morning light.
They flip and they flop, with syrup they glide,
Whispers of sweetness, in butter they hide.

A fork in my hand, a dilemma so grand,
Should I eat now, or save a few for the band?
But once they are gone, I'm left with regrets,
Life's like a pancake—it's filled with odd debts.

Stacked like my dreams, but flat in between,
Each layer a hope, some crispy, some lean.
With laughter and crumbs, they fill up my plate,
Who knew breakfast could help me contemplate?

So here's to the moments, both silken and rough,
In butter and syrup, we find out what's tough.
With each little bite, I ponder my fate,
Should I hurry or linger? It's all on my plate.

Cooking Up Contemplation

The griddle's alive, with a sizzling song,
Pouring the batter, it can't be wrong.
Each bubble that rises, a thought on the way,
Flipping my worries, they melt in the fray.

What makes life so round? Is it syrup or cream?
Or maybe the laughter that rolls like a dream?
Eggs in the mix, oh what a delight,
With spatulas dancing, we twirl into night.

The spatula's wisdom, so simple yet grand,
It teaches me patience with a flick of the hand.
And though I may stumble, I rise with the cake,
In the world of the batter, there's much to partake.

So serve up your whims, let them float on the heat,
For every great notion deserves a sweet treat.
With laughter a'cooking, and joy on the flame,
Each pancake I serve has its own little name.

Buttering Dreams

A pat of sheer joy, on a fluffy delight,
Sister of syrup, and cousin of bright.
With rhythms of breakfast, I find my own tune,
Dance like a pancake, beneath the full moon.

An apron of hope, on my waist it is tied,
Flinging flour like confetti, with nowhere to hide.
The more that I whisk, the clearer it gets,
Dreams are like pancakes; don't worry, no debts.

With bananas and chocolate, I twirl and I spin,
Each flap of the batter, my spirits begin.
Gather 'round the table, with forks at the ready,
Life's batter is thick, but my laughter is steady.

So butter those dreams, as they sizzle and flip,
Embrace the absurd, take a chance, take a trip.
In the pool of the morning, let laughter consume,
For every warm pancake brings joy to the room.

Circles of Intention

Round and round, like a pancake's grace,
Life's little circles, all fall into place.
With jelly and jam, I spread out my cheer,
Each syrupy swirl whispers, 'Dreams all draw near.'

The spatula spins tales, both silly and wise,
A flip of intention, right under the skies.
So gather your toppings, let flavors collide,
In the kitchen of chaos, let laughter reside.

Each meal is a quest, each bite a delight,
With friends at my table, everything's right.
We chat and we giggle, with pancakes galore,
Every fluffy circle just opens the door.

So let's flip the norm, with joyful intent,
And savor the moments that breakfast has lent.
With plates all around, and hearts open wide,
In circles of laughter, let's all take a ride.

Lifting the Weight of Flapjacks

Pancakes piled high like dreams on a plate,
Each syrupy layer helps me contemplate.
Do I flip for fortune or just for the fun?
Too many cooks? Nah, I'm the chosen one!

With every pancake, wisdom starts to rise,
But calories whisper sweet little lies.
Do I work out harder or just give in?
This pancake life makes me grin and spin!

In this fluffy world, the spatula reigns,
While butter and laughter course through my veins.
Stacking my worries? I do it with glee,
One flip at a time, it's pancake therapy!

So here's to the griddle, my dear friend so warm,
When life gets too heavy, it's time for the charm.
With a sprinkle of joy and a dash of light fate,
I rise like the pancakes, it's never too late!

Whisking Through Realization

With a whisk in my hand, I ponder my fate,
Mixing my dreams, oh isn't it great?
Each stir brings a chuckle, a giggle, a cheer,
Maybe pancakes hold secrets I'm meant to hear.

I toss in some laughter, and sprinkle some fun,
Fried in a skillet, we bask in the sun.
A pinch of confusion, a tablespoon of flair,
Stirring life's mix, flavors floating in air!

The batter's a metaphor, isn't that neat?
Sometimes you stumble, but don't miss a beat.
I'll fry up my worries in golden delight,
Each pancake a lesson, each morning a bite!

So here's to the kitchen where wisdom meets zest,
Whisking away what puts us to rest.
Life's but a pancake, so flip it with style,
Let's serve it up sunny, and stay for a while!

Toppings of Thoughtfulness

Maple syrup dreams drizzled thick with a grin,
Picking toppings like choices, where do I begin?
Chocolate chips giggle, they know they are sweet,
Strawberries whisper, 'Come, join us for a treat!'

Each choice a decision, like berries or cream,
Life's little toppings, they make the heart beam.
Do I go fancy or simple instead?
Life's a buffet—so much love on the spread!

A dollop of laughter, a swirl of delight,
Yogurt or whipped cream, oh, which one feels right?
Every layer has lessons, they make my heart race,
With a generous serving, I find my own space!

So top off your pancakes with kindness and cheer,
Let every bite spark joy year after year.
In this pancake journey, let's gather around,
For each topping we choose, is a treasure we've found!

Simmering Secrets

In the heat of the kitchen, ideas start to bubble,
Secrets simmer gently, disguised in the rubble.
As pancakes sizzle, my thoughts swirl and dance,
In this crispy chaos, I find my romance.

What's hidden beneath that fluffy veneer?
Might be wisdom or wonder; let's give it a cheer!
With a spatula ready, I flip with a smile,
Each turn tells a story, let's linger a while!

So cue up the syrup, let moments unfold,
As secrets fill kitchens, special and bold.
In this bubbling pot of pancake delight,
Let's sip on our dreams and toast to the night!

The world may be messy, but nothing can beat,
The joy of a pancake, a life that's so sweet.
So let's gather our friends for a flip and a cheer,
For the secrets we share, and the laughter we hear!

www.ingramcontent.com/pod-product-compliance
Lightning Source LLC
Chambersburg PA
CBHW070751220426
43209CB00083B/738